HORIZONS

Learning to Read

Level A
Textbook 3

Siegfried Engelmann
Owen Engelmann
Karen Lou Seitz Davis

SRA McGraw-Hill

Columbus, Ohio

A Division of The McGraw-Hill Companies

Illustration Credits

Dave Blanchette, Cindy Brodie, Daniel Clifford, Mark Corcoran, Susanne Demarco, Pam Faessler, Frank Ferri, Kersti Frigell, Simon Galkin, Ethel Gold, Dara Goldman, Meryl Henderson, Gay Holland, Ann Iosa, Susan Jerde, Anne Kennedy, Loretta Lustig, Margaret San Filippo, Pat Schories, Jeff Severn, Charles Shaw, Lauren Simeone, Lucia Washburn, Lane Yerkes.

SRA/McGraw-Hill

*A Division of The **McGraw·Hill** Companies*

Printed in the United States of America.

Send all inquiries to:
SRA/McGraw-Hill
8787 Orion Place
Columbus, OH 43240-4027

ISBN 0-02-674192-X

2 3 4 5 6 7 8 9 VHJ 01

p b t k

d u n t v k g

1. hug
2. run
3. up

1. was 2. to 3. said
4. do

1. hear
2. hope
3. greet
4. land
5. go

1. stones
2. miles
3. kissed

1

An ant said, "I need to go home." It was five miles to his home. A crow said, "I can take you home. Hold my tail and we will fly."

In no time, the crow and the ant came over an ant hill. The ant told the crow to land. And the ant gave the crow a kiss.

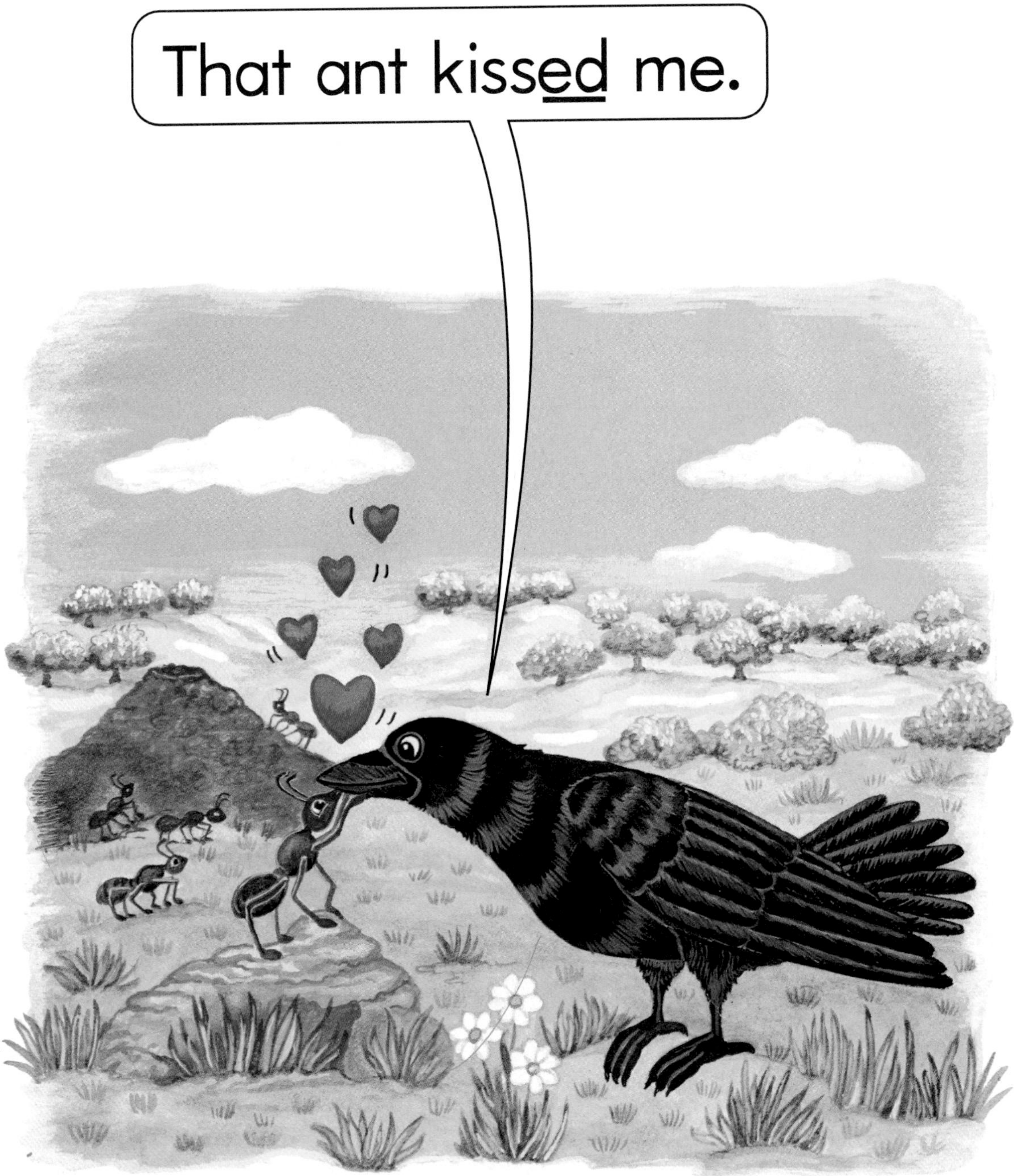
That ant kissed me.

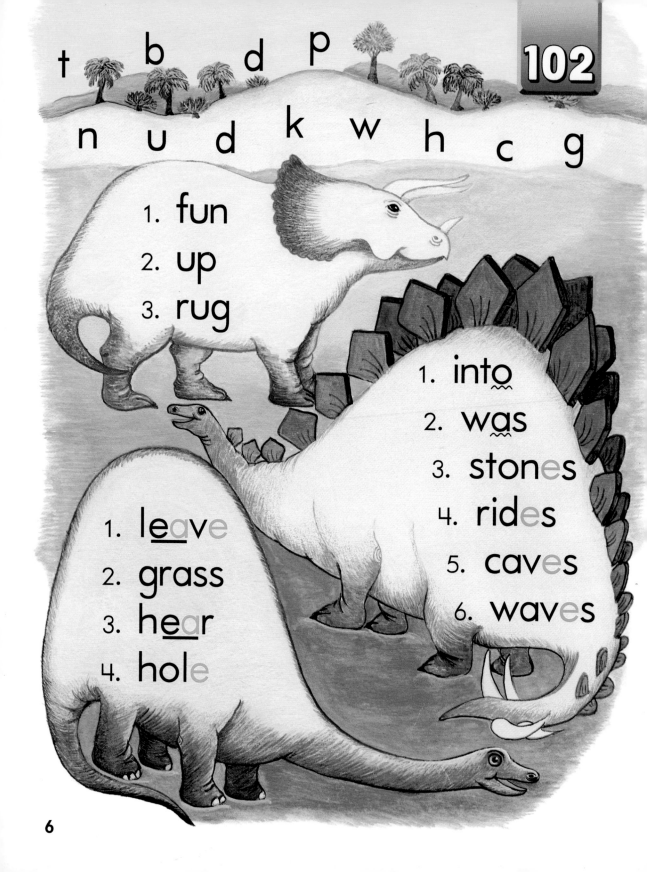

t b d p

n u d k w h c g

1. fun
2. up
3. rug

1. into
2. was
3. stones
4. rides
5. caves
6. waves

1. leave
2. grass
3. hear
4. hole

6

A seal said, "I like to ride waves."

That seal was in waves near caves. The seal will ride a wave into a cave. The wave will take the seal over stones.

Will the seal like the ride? No. The ride will make the seal sore.

b d c b v

h b g c b u

1. here
2. hole
3. le**a**ve
4. st**ay**
5. slid
6. into

some
from

1. mud
2. dug
3. sun

A mole had a fine home. That home was in a hole. A toad came into the home. The mole said, "Leave my home."

The toad said, "No. I like it and I will stay."

The mole said, "If you stay, I will go."

And he did.

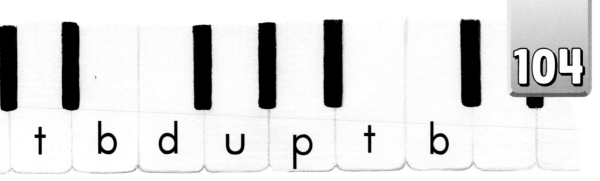

t b d u p t b

1. pl**ay**<u>ed</u>
2. st**ay**<u>ed</u>
3. slid
4. dry

1. by
2. big
3. rub

1. from
2. s<u>o</u>me
3. won

1. sun
2. fun
3. w**ay**
4. h**ay**

Five cats had fun at a lake. 2 cats played with a mole. 2 cats ran up a hill.

1 cat slid into the lake.

Do cats like to play in a lake? No. Cats like to stay dry.

So the cat ran from the lake and sat in the sun.

Five cats had fun at a lake. 2 cats pl_ay_ed with a mole. 2 cats ran up a hill.

1 cat slid into the lake.
Do cats like to play in a lake? No. Cats like to stay dry.

So the cat ran from the lake and sat in the sun.

u h b d h w b

oa

ay

1. but
2. big
3. grab
4. rub

1. some
2. said
3. was
4. do
5. from
6. into

1. hide
2. hid
3. hay
4. know
5. keep

20

A pig had a coat. The goat ate that coat. The pig said, "I am cold."

The goat said, "I know a way to keep the cold from you."

The goat told the pig, "Go to that hay pile and hide in it."

So the pig hid in the hay.

I know a way to keep the cold from you. Go hide in the hay.

b h u d p b g

oa
ai

1. grab
2. dig
3. big

1. of
2. done
3. some
4. come

1. Al
2. pal
3. named
4. tail

1. stick
2. we
3. fly
4. kite
5. these

An ant named Al told his pals, "We can fly."

These pals said, "No, no, no."

Al said, "Stay with me and you will see."

Al and his pals ran to a kite. Al said, "Grab the tail and we will fly."

The kite sailed over the trees. The ants said, "We can fly."

ay ai ea d u h b

107

can't
didn't
don't

1. sick
2. stick
3. tape
4. dime
5. mud
6. pay

1. have
2. asked
3. last
4. but

1. of
2. done
3. come
4. from

29

An old man asked a crow, "Will you pay a dime for a coat?"

The old man said, "No goat will eat that coat. It will stick to you."

The crow gave the man a dime. The man gave the crow a coat made of tape.

The crow said, "I can't fly."

The old man said, "But you can run." And the crow did.

Will you pay a dime for this coat?

h   b   w   ea   ai   th   g

can't
don't
didn't

1. Bob
2. have
3. asked
4. last
5. by

1. but
2. mud
3. must
4. jump

1. come
2. of
3. from
4. done

The Hill of Mud
Part 1

Bob asked his dad, "Can I go for a hike with my pals?"

His dad said, "You may go, but you have to stay near the path. And you have to come home by five."

Bob and his pals hiked for 3 miles. At last a pal said, "I see a hill of mud."

More to come.

Can I go for a hike with my pals?

You may go, but you have to stay near the path. And you have to come home by five.

th   ck   ai   ea   oa

1. it's
2. didn't
3. don't

1. thing   2. these
3. big   4. be

1. <u>o</u>th<u>er</u>
2. hav<u>e</u>
3. <u>of</u>
4. <u>ea</u>rs
5. t<u>ea</u>rs

1. st<u>ay</u><u>ed</u>
2. <u>p</u>l<u>ay</u><u>ed</u>
3. fast
4. last
5. <u>c</u><u>o</u>me
6. s<u>o</u>m<u>e</u>

The Hill of Mud
Part 2

A pal said, "We can play in that big hill of mud."

Bob said, "But we have to stay near the path."

The pals said, "You stay. We will play."

But Bob didn't stay. He played in mud. At last some of his pals said, "It is time to go home."

Bob didn't hear his pals. Bob had mud in his ears.

More to come.

wh th ck ay ea oa

<u>wh</u>y
<u>whil</u>e

1. div<u>e</u>
2. hiv<u>e</u>
3. mor<u>e</u>
4. sor<u>e</u>

1. tal<u>e</u>
2. bik<u>e</u>
3. back
4. s<u>ea</u>
5. thing

1. <u>other</u>
2. be
3. by
4. <u>t</u><u>ea</u>rs

it's
can't

The Hill of Mud
Part 3

Bob played and played.
At last some of his pals told
him, "It's late. You must run
to be home by five."

As Bob ran home, a man
said, "I see a hill of mud that
can run."

Bob made it home by five.
His dad said, "But you didn't
stay near the path." So Bob
can't hike with his pals for
some time.

> The end.

It's late. You must run to be home by five.

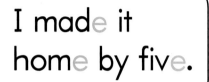

th wh g b h j d

1. g<u>ea</u>r
2. r<u>ea</u>r
3. h<u>ea</u>r
4. dry
5. cry

<u>wh</u>eel
<u>wh</u>il<u>e</u>
<u>wh</u>y

1. tal s
2. rode
3. s<u>ea</u>
4. waves
5. sore
6. bik s

1. things 2. bug
3. back 4. fill<u>ed</u>

48

We Like That

We can hike and we can bike.
And we can do things that we like.
We may play and we may run.
Or we may read to have some fun.
If it is dry, we can bike to the sea.
We see big waves as we sit near a tree.
We come back home filled with tales
Of stones and waves and sea and sails.

We Like That

We can hike and we can bike.
And we can do things that we like.

We may play and we may run.
Or we may read to have some fun.
If it is dry, we can bike to the sea.
We see big waves as we sit near a tree.

We come back home filled with tales
Of stones and waves and sea and sails.

d p b g th wh ay

wheel
why
while

1. tear
2. gear
3. rear
4. dear
5. hear

1. rode
2. bee
3. Ann
4. some
5. sore

1. hive
2. games
3. bikes
4. bug

Dear Dad,
   The other day we rode bikes to a lake. We ate and played games. I had my gear near a bee hive. Bees gave me some tears. I have a sore ear, but I can hear. And I have a sore rear. So I can't sit. And I can't ride my bike for a while.

                    From Ann

Note to Dad

Dear Dad,
    The other day we rode bikes to a lake. We ate and played games.

I had my g<u>ea</u>r n<u>ea</u>r a bee hive. Bees gave me s<u>o</u>me t<u>ea</u>rs.

I have a sore ear, but I can 113
hear. And I have a sore
rear. So I can't sit. And I
can't ride my bike for a while.
From Ann

ar

ar

wh d u th b ar ck w

1. home
2. this
3. while
4. holes
5. hat

1. at
2. w<u>ai</u>t
3. rode
4. t<u>oa</u>d
5. jok
6. s<u>oa</u>k

1. <u>ea</u>t
2. at
3. bugs
4. jump

The Bug and the Toad

A toad had a fine home. A mean bug dug a big hole into the home.

The toad said, "This is my home. Don't make holes in it."

The bug said, "I can make holes if I feel like it."

The toad said, "And I can eat bugs if I feel like it."

And the toad did that.

The end.

ar

oa

ai

ea

ar

ay

1. w<u>ai</u>t
2. c<u>oa</u>t
3. l<u>ea</u>p
4. s<u>oa</u>k
5. h<u>ea</u>r
6. r<u>ai</u>ns

1. <u>a</u>rm
2. f<u>a</u>rm
3. b<u>a</u>rn

to
do
who

1. blow
2. jump
3. wind
4. lick
5. it's

63

I Wait for My Pal

I hate to wait. But I have to sit and wait while it rains.

I w<u>ai</u>t for my pal, the m<u>ai</u>l man.

The r<u>ai</u>n has made him late. That r<u>ai</u>n will s<u>oa</u>k my c<u>oa</u>t and my t<u>ai</u>l, but I will sit in the r<u>ai</u>n.

At last I h<u>ear</u> him and see him. I will jump up. It's time for us to have some fun.

ay th oa ar ai p b d

who
do

1. b_rn
2. _rt
3. st_rt

1. three
2. rug
3. stick
4. stove
5. but

1. awa_y
2. fire
3. last
4. flame

1. c_ar
2. f_ar
3. dry
4. sky

Fun with My Pal

I sat in the r<u>ai</u>n, but at last my pal came home. We had fun as we pl<u>ay</u>ed with a stick. We pl<u>ay</u>ed in the r<u>ai</u>n.

He told me it was time to eat. We ate near the stove in his home.

At last I am dry. So I go to the rug. I can h<u>ear</u> the r<u>ai</u>n, but I am dry. And it is time for me to sleep.

ea   ai   oa   ay   ar   wh   th

1. began
2. aw<u>ay</u>
3. bad
4. hold
5. f<u>ar</u>m
6. b<u>ar</u>n

1. <u>ear</u>
2. t<u>ea</u>r
3. <u>are</u>
4. f<u>ar</u>

1. who
2. wind
3. three
4. flames
5. fire
6. blow

A Mean Wind
Part 1

A mean wind made three pals cold. So the pals made a fire near a farm. The mean wind said, "I will blow and make that fire big." The wind made flames leap way up.

The pals said, "We have to keep this fire from the barn." But the pals didn't hold the fire. And in no time, that fire was near the barn.

More to come.

A Mean Wind
Part 1

A mean wind made three pals
cold. So the pals made a fire near a
farm.

The mean wind said, "I will blow and make that fire big." The wind made flames leap way up.

The pals said, "We have to keep this fire from the barn." But the pals didn't hold the fire. And in no time, that fire was near the barn.

sh   sh   ay   ar

wh

sh   th

1. <u>a</u>re
2. r<u>ea</u>r
3. r<u>oa</u>r
4. <u>a</u>rm
5. f<u>ea</u>r

1. <u>wh</u>at
2. aw<u>ay</u>
3. side
4. lick

1. said
2. you
3. was
4. to

1. sky
2. ho ho
3. bad
4. slid

A Mean Wind
Part 2

A mean wind made a fire leap over to a barn. The wind made a bad joke. The wind said, "Ho ho. It's time for a barn fire."

The pals said, "If we don't hold this fire, the barn will go up in flames."

The mean wind said, "You can't keep these flames away from the barn." And the wind made the fire jump up and lick at the barn.

More to come.

h sh s ea wh

sh

1. f**ea**r
2. f**ar**
3. t**ea**r
4. t**ar**

1. **wh**at
2. on
3. began
4. aw**ay**
5. just

1. won't
2. sid**e**
3. slid**e**
4. sky
5. s**oa**k
6. miss

1. wi**sh**
2. fi**sh**
3. **sh**e

81

A M<u>ea</u>n Wind
P<u>ar</u>t Three

The m<u>ea</u>n wind said, "I will blow
big flames up the side <u>of</u> that b<u>ar</u>n."
But as the flames began to l<u>ea</u>p
up the side <u>of</u> the b<u>ar</u>n, r<u>ai</u>n came
from the sky.

82

The rain said to the mean wind, "I will keep those flames away from the barn."

In no time, the fire was no more.

The rain told the wind, "Leave this
farm or I will soak you some more."
The pals said, "We like rain."
But the mean wind said, "I hate rain."

The end.

b   h   th   sh   wh   ea

or

1. <u>sh</u>ip
2. <u>sh</u>ow
3. wi<u>sh</u>
4. <u>sh</u>e

1. <u>wh</u>at
2. who
3. on
4. no
5. rug
6. h<u>ar</u>d

1. slide
2. slid
3. hate
4. hat
5. fast
6. won't

The Fast Rug
Part 1

A hard rain made mud on a hill. A pig told a goat, "We can have some fun on that hill. We can sit in the mud and slide."

The g<u>oa</u>t said, "But we will hav<u>e</u> mud on us. I don't like mud."

The pig said, "I hav<u>e</u> a rug. We can sit on the rug. That rug will slid<u>e</u> on the mud. And we won't hav<u>e</u> mud on us."

So the g<u>oa</u>t and the pig sat on
that rug. The pig said, "Hold on."
And the rug slid on the mud. The
g<u>oa</u>t said, "This rug is fast."

More to come.

h   w   s   sh

1. <u>s</u>he
2. <u>s</u>hip
3. ca<u>sh</u>

ring
sing

1. to
2. too
3. do
4. und<u>er</u>
5. o

1. snak
2. land
3. slid
4. stuck
5. free
6. still

1. miss
2. on
3. <u>s</u>ail<u>ed</u>

The Fast Rug
Part 2

A goat and a pig sat on a rug.
That rug slid on the side of a hill.
It slid fast. The goat said, "A tree
is in the way."

A tree is in
the way.

The pig said, "We will miss that tree." But the rug ran into that tree. The g<u>oa</u>t and the pig s<u>ai</u>l<u>ed</u> into the sky. <u>Wh</u><u>a</u>t did the pals land in? Mud, mud, mud.

Oh dear.

The g<u>oa</u>t said, "I hat<u>e</u> mud, but we hav<u>e</u> mud on us. So we can slid<u>e</u> on the mud s<u>o</u>me mor<u>e</u>." Did the pals d<u>o</u> that? Yes.

Weeeee.

w h s t sh wh th

1. sham
2. cash
3. wish

1. have
2. stuck
3. free
4. still
5. spoke
6. oh

1. to
2. too
3. two
4. won't
5. the big one
6. wise

sing
bring
thing

The Mole and the Crow
Part 1

Moles can't see. A mole dug a hole and ran into a tree. The mole asked the tree, "Who are you?" The tree was still.

A crow was in the tree. That crow said, "I will have some fun with that mole."

The crow said, "Oh, mole. You
have run into me. I am the big one.
And I am stuck in the mud. Can you
dig and free my feet?"

"I don't know," the mole said.
"But I will try."

More to come.

g   b   d   sh   th   wh

1. these
2. while
3. will
4. snake
5. think

shine
fish
she

1. two
2. wise
3. from

1. her
2. were
3. other
4. mother

1. playing
2. trying
3. digging

The Mole and the Crow
Part Two

A crow told the mole what to do. And the mole began to dig. The mole dug and dug. At last, the mole said, "I dig, dig, dig, but these feet are big, big, big."

As the mole dug, she came to the home of a wise old snake. The snake said, "Why do you dig into the side of my home?"

The mole said, "I need to free these big feet from the mud."

"What big feet?" the snake asked. The mole told the snake.

More to come.

I dig, dig, dig, but these feet are big, big, big.

Why do you dig into the side of my home?

I need to free these big feet.

er   sh   th   wh
ai   ar   ay

1. from
2. of
3. for
4. free

w<u>e</u>r<u>e</u>
h<u>er</u>
und<u>er</u>

1. trying
2. pl<u>ay</u>ing
3. digging

<u>sh</u>ow
<u>sh</u>ame
ca<u>sh</u>

1. think
2. thing
3. lump
4. gold

The Mole and the Crow
Part Three

The mole was trying to free feet. The mole dug into the home of a wise old snake. The snake told the mole, "You think you are digging under the big one. But you are digging under a tree."

The mole said, "But the big one told me what to do."

"No," the snake said. "Some one is playing a joke."

"What can I do?" the mole asked.

The snake smiled and said, "I think I know what to do. We can play jokes, too. And I think I know a fine joke."

More to come.

The big one told me what to do.

Some one is playing a joke.

sh th wh er or b g w

1. top   2. on
3. not   4. now

1. going   2. raining
3. under 4. were 5. other

1. became
2. four
3. gold
4. lump
5. dark
6. teeth

waited
darted
started

What did you s<u>ay</u>?

The Mol<u>e</u> and the Crow
P<u>ar</u>t 4

The wis<u>e</u> old snak<u>e</u> told the mol<u>e</u> <u>wh</u>at to do. The mol<u>e</u> cam<u>e</u> from the hole. <u>Sh</u>e said to the crow, "Oh, big <u>o</u>n<u>e</u>, I can't free feet that <u>ar</u>e stuck in gold."

"<u>Wh</u>at did you s<u>ay</u>?" the crow ask<u>ed</u>.

The mole told the crow, "Just go
into the hole I was digging, and you will
see gold."

So the crow slid into the hole the
mole had dug. At last the crow came
to a lump of gold.

One part to go.

i a o

1. lot
2. how
3. not
4. stop

st<u>ar</u>t<u>ed</u>
d<u>ar</u>t<u>ed</u>
hat<u>ed</u>

1. spok<u>e</u>
2. <u>sh</u>am<u>e</u>
3. d<u>ar</u>k
4. becam<u>e</u>
5. pl<u>ay</u>ing
6. grab

1. teeth
2. sing
3. think

The Mole and the Crow
Part Five

"I see gold," the crow said. She was in the hole. As she started to grab for the gold, it became dark. The crow didn't know it, but the gold was one of the snake's gold teeth.

The snake spoke like the big one.
"Oh, bad crow," he said. "Shame on
you for playing mean jokes."

The crow darted from the hole. As she started to fly away, she said to the mole, "You can have the gold."

That was the last joke the crow played on moles.

The end.

o th er sh ar

1. end**ed**
2. land**ed**
3. need**ed**

1. got
2. lot
3. cow
4. now

1. wins
2. w**ai**ting
3. eating
4. singing
5. fast**er**

1. corn
2. Jan
3. greet
4. ov**er**
5. m**o**th**er**
6. aw**ay**

What Jan Sings

Jan liked to sing, but she made her mother sick of her singing.

One day her mother spoke to Jan. Her mother said, "I like the way you sing, but you sing the same thing over and over. Can you sing other things?"

Jan said, "I like to sing the same thing."

Her mother said, "I will do some thing for you if you sing more than one thing. What can I do for you?"

Jan said, "Will you sing with me?"

Jan's mom said, "Yes."

Now Jan and her mother sing lots of fine things. If you are near Jan's home, you can hear that singing.

The end.

What Jan Sings

Jan liked to sing, but she made her mother sick of her singing.

One day her mother spoke to Jan. Her mother said, "I like the way you sing, but you sing the same thing over and over. Can you sing other things?"

Jan said, "I like to sing the same thing."

Her mother said, "I will do some thing for you if you sing more than one thing. What can I do for you?"

Jan said, "Will you sing with me?"

Jan's mom said, "Yes."

Now Jan and her mother sing lots of fine things. If you are near Jan's home, you can hear that singing.

The end.

o   oa   er   ar   th   sh

1. got   2. cow   3. <u>sh</u>op

1. end<u>ed</u>
2. hat<u>ed</u>
3. hand<u>ed</u>

1. wins
2. eating
3. fast<u>er</u>
4. thinks
5. lat<u>er</u>

1. corn
2. leap
3. over
4. away
5. these

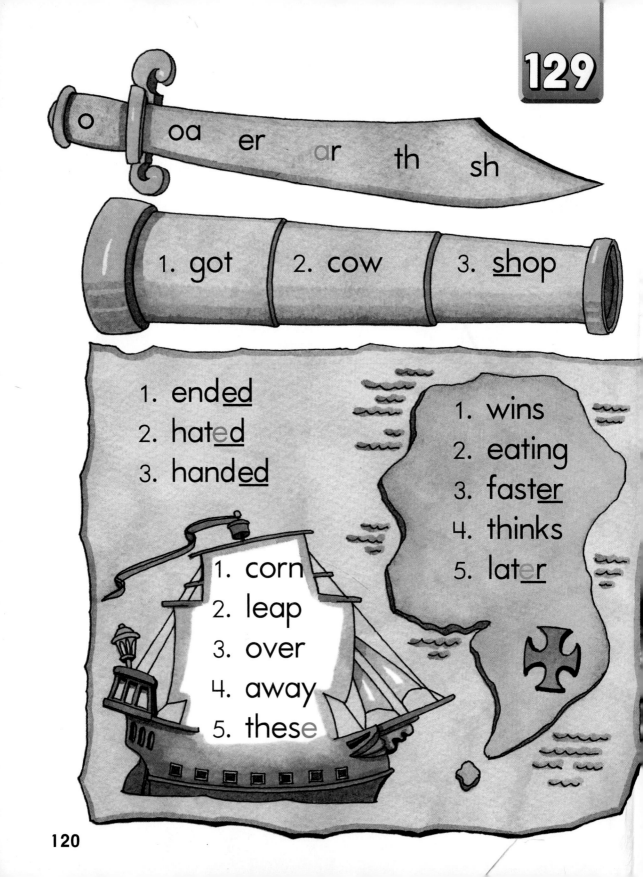

Eating Corn

A pig and a goat liked to eat.
One day, the goat and the pig were
near a pile of corn.

The goat said, "I can eat that pile of
corn."

The pig said, "Me too."

The goat got mad and said, "I can
eat faster than you."

Now the pig said, "You can not."

A cow said, "<u>Why</u> don't you st<u>a</u>rt eating and see who wins?"

So the g<u>oa</u>t and the pig st<u>a</u>r<u>ted</u> to eat the corn.

The cow said, "I think I will eat, too." And <u>she</u> did.

Who ate more corn? The cow.
Who ate faster? The cow.
Who got mad? The pig and the goat.

The end.

ai ea oa ar ay

i o a

1. cop
2. hop
3. <u>sh</u>op
4. top
5. stop

1. b<u>ur</u>n
2. st<u>ir</u>
3. f<u>ir</u>st
4. b<u>ir</u>d

1. b_rking
2. hearing
3. waiting
4. l<u>ea</u>ving

er
ir
ur

1. made
2. late
3. hate
4. time
5. while

1. wait
2. rain
3. mail
4. tail

1. soak
2. coat

Waiting for a Pal

I hate to wait. I hate to sit in the rain. But I have to sit and wait while it rains.

I wait for my pal. My pal is the mail man.

The rain has made him late. That rain will soak my coat and my tail, but I will sit in the rain and wait.

At last I hear him and see him.
I will run and jump. It's time for us
to have lots of fun.

The end.

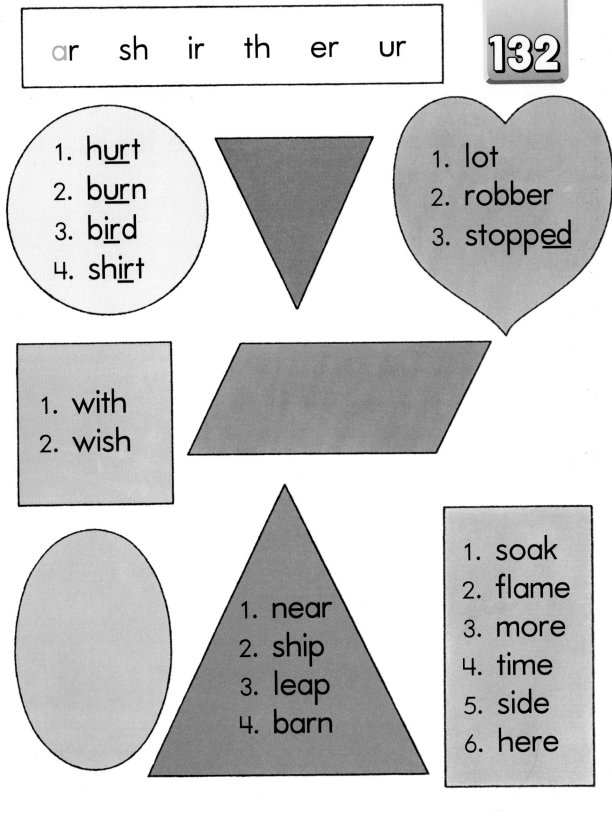

1. hu**r**t
2. bu**r**n
3. b**ir**d
4. sh**ir**t

1. lot
2. robber
3. stopp**ed**

1. with
2. wish

1. near
2. ship
3. leap
4. barn

1. soak
2. flame
3. more
4. time
5. side
6. here

A Mean Wind

Three pals made a fire near a farm. A mean wind made that fire leap over to the barn. The mean wind said, "I will blow big flames up the side of that barn."

But just as the flames began to leap up the side of the barn, rain came from the sky. Here is what the rain said to the mean wind, "I will keep those flames away from the barn."

In no time, the fire was no more.

The rain told the wind, "Leave this farm or I will soak you some more."

The pals said, "We like rain."

But the mean wind said, "I hate rain."

This is the end.

a i o

1. firm
2. hurt
3. shirt
4. dirt

1. shop
2. hot
3. stopped

1. robber
2. hiding
3. landed
4. rings
5. sneak

1. slide
2. what
3. goat
4. smiled
5. some
6. hit

The Fast Rug

A hill had mud on it. A pig told a goat, "We can sit on my rug and slide on that hill. The rug will keep mud away from us."

So the goat and the pig sat on that rug. And the rug slid on the mud. A tree was in the way, and the rug hit the tree. The goat and the pig sailed into the sky and landed in the mud.

The goat said, "Now we have mud on us. So we can slide on the mud some more."

And that is what the goat and the pig did.

Weeeee.

k   x   y

ir   ur

sh   wh   ea   o   a   i

1. Pam
2. lump
3. lamp
4. sn<u>ea</u>k
5. hidi<u>ng</u>

1. cop
2. rock
3. clock

1. li<u>ttl</u>e
2. t<u>ur</u><u>tl</u>e
3. bitt<u>er</u>
4. robbers

1. rings
2. hunt
3. plan

Pam and the Gold Robber
Part One

Pam had a ship. She lived on that ship. In her ship, she had a shop. The shop was filled with lots of things.

One thing in that shop was lots of
gold. Pam made gold rings and
other gold things from the gold.
But that gold was not in a big lump.
Pam made the gold into some thing
you see in a shop. That was her
way of hiding the gold. She said,
"My gold is now safe from robbers."

But <u>o</u>ne d<u>ay</u> a robber said, "I will sn<u>ea</u>k into that ship and take the gold from h<u>er</u> shop."

This is not the end.

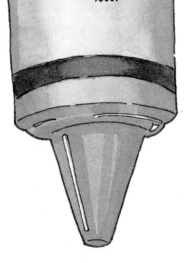

1. butt**er**
2. bitt**er**
3. lat**er**
4. aft**er**
5. litt**le**

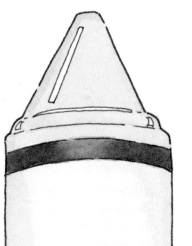

1. cops
2. down
3. rocks
4. clocks

1. pick
2. sacks
3. lamp
4. plan
5. hunt

1. hid**ing**
2. leav**ing**
3. grabb**ed**

Pam and the Gold Robber
Part Two

A robber had a plan. He was going to sneak into Pam's ship and take her gold. He did not know that she had hid her gold. She had made the gold into some thing in her shop.

The robber got into his little boat.
He waited as the sky got dark. He
started to go to Pam's ship.

At last, he came to the ship. He said, "Now I will go up the side of this ship and sneak into Pam's shop."

The robber did that. It was dark and still in the shop. The robber said, "Now I will hunt for the gold."

More next time.

1. bitt**er**
2. batt**er**
3. butt**er**
4. aft**er**
5. t**u**r**t**le
6. l**ea**ving

1.   ow
2.   how
3.   brown
4.   town
5.   down
6.   mom

1.   **sho**w
2.   throw
3.   cl**ea**n
4.   pick·
5.   sacks

Pam and the Gold Robber
Part Three

Pam had a shop on h<u>er</u> ship. A robber got into h<u>er</u> shop to take the gold.

He said, "I see sacks and rocks and clocks. And I see a big lamp. But I see no gold."

At last, he gave up. Just as he was leaving, two cops came and grabbed him.

Later, the cops asked Pam, "Can you show us how you hide the gold?"

She said, "If you pick up the big lamp, you will know how I hide the gold."

One cop grabb<u>ed</u> the lamp. He
said, "I can't pick up this lamp."

The <u>other</u> cop said, "I know <u>why</u>
you can't pick it up. It's made of gold.
Ho, ho, ho."

The end.

c s x sh

1. down
2. town
3. things
4. bring
5. mom
6. clean

1. taste
2. bake
3. cake
4. sweet
5. luck
6. dirt

fox
fix
mix

Sid Cleans Up the Town

Sid liked things that were clean. But the town he lived in had lots of dirt.

Sid told his mom, "I will make this town cl<u>ea</u>n."

His mom ask<u>ed</u>, "How will you do that?"

Sid said, "I will make it rain. The rain will cl<u>ea</u>n the d<u>ir</u>t away."

"But how will you make it rain?"

Sid said, "I will sing. What I sing will bring rain."

His mom said, "I don't think singing will make rain."

What I sing will bring rain.

I don't think so.

But Sid st<u>ar</u>t<u>ed</u> to sing. In a litt<u>le</u> while, the sky got d<u>ar</u>k and lots of rain came down.

Sid's mom said, "I do not know what to think now."

Sid smil<u>e</u>d and said, "I think the town is cl<u>ea</u>n now."

And it was.

The end.

x   er   sh   ur   wh   ir

fox
box
mix

1. stopped
2. after
3. cake
4. luck
5. back

1. throw
2. brown
3. cash
4. taste

1. sweet
2. turtles
3. baked
4. batter

151

Bitter Butter
Part One

A little turtle asked her mom to bake a cake. Her mom said, "We will need butter for the batter. So go to the farm and bring back some sweet butter."

She gave the little turtle some cash.

As the little t<u>ur</u>tle got near the farm, a brown fox stopped her. The fox asked her, "What do you plan to do with that ca<u>sh</u>?"

The little t<u>ur</u>tle told the fox that she needed sweet butter. The fox said, "You <u>are</u> in luck. I have some sweet butter." But the butter the fox had was bitter butter.

After the little turtle was on her way home,
the fox said, "Ho ho. Now I do not have to
throw that bitter butter away."

This is not the end.

ch wh th sh

next box mixed

1. story
2. happy
3. funny

1. something
2. visit
3. waited
4. showed
5. won't
6. done

1. tasted
2. turn
3. sold
4. real
5. bitter

Bitter Butter

Part Two

The brown fox had sold some bitter butter to
the little turtle. Later, the little turtle came home
with that butter.

Her mom showed her how to make a cake.
Her mom said, "You start with a cake batter."

Her mom began to make the batter. She said, "We mix sweet butter into the batter." But the butter she had was not sweet. It was bitter. And bitter butter won't make a sweet cake.

After the batter was made, the turtles waited while the cake baked. At last it was done.

The little turtle asked, "Can I taste that cake?"

"Yes," her mom said, and gave the little turtle some cake.

The little turtle tasted the cake and said, "Yuk."

More to come.

ch   sh   th   wh

1. wore
2. I'm
3. I've
4. pay
5. turn

1. only
2. tiny
3. funny
4. story
5. really

1. next
2. visit
3. drink
4. pond
5. first
6. six

1. something
2. someone

Bitter Butter
P<u>ar</u>t Three

The little turtle tast<u>e</u>d the cake. Did she like the tast<u>e</u>? No. She said, "Mom, this cake is not sweet. It is bitter."

Her mom said, "How can the cake be bitter? The batter has fine things in it."

Her mom tast<u>e</u>d the cake and said, "Yuk. That cake is bitter."

Her mom started to think. After a while she said, "Something bitter got into the cake batter. I think it was the butter. Bitter butter makes the batter bitter."

The little turtle's mom asked, "Who sold you this butter?"

"The brown fox," the little turtle said.

Her mom said, "We will go back and see him. I have something to say to him."

> More next time.

sh   ch   x   c   s   k

1. each
2. beach
3. chase

1. mother
2. another
3. visited
4. pond
5. dove
6. drink

1. nearly
2. dirty
3. really

someone
something

1. swim
2. thinking
3. kids
4. glad

Bitter Butter
Part Four

The next d<u>ay</u>, the m<u>o</u>ther turtle and the little
turtle visited the brown fox. The turtles had a big
cake.

The mother turtle told the fox, "We have a cake for you, but you have to <u>sh</u>ow us that you like cake."

The fox lik<u>e</u>d things that w<u>ere</u> free, so he said, "I like it, I like it."

"You told us you like it," the mother turtle said. "But you have to <u>sho</u>w us that you like it."

"How can I do that?" the fox asked.

The mother turtle said, "If you eat some cake really fast, we will know that you like it."

"I can do that," the fox said.

More to come.

x

th   ch   sh

1. baby
2. only
3. easy
4. nearly
5. body

1. shop
2. chop
3. wish
4. which

1. why
2. dove
3. I'm
4. wore
5. drink
6. visited

1. beat
2. began
3. sitting

Bitter Butter
Part Five

The mother turtle gave the fox some cake.
He ate it so fast that he didn't taste how bitter it was.
But after he was done, it started to leave a bad
taste.

"Did you like that?" the mother turtle asked.

"I . . . I . . ." the fox said. "I . . . need
something to drink."

The fox ran to the pond and dove in. He began
to drink and drink, but the bad bitter taste did not
go away.

"That cake is bitter," the fox said at last.

The mom said, "Do you know why?"

The fox said, "Oh, it must be the butter I
sold you."

The mother turtle said, "Yes, that bitter butter made the batter bitter."

The fox said, "And that bitter batter gave me a bitter taste."

That was the last time the fox sold someone bitter butter.

The end.

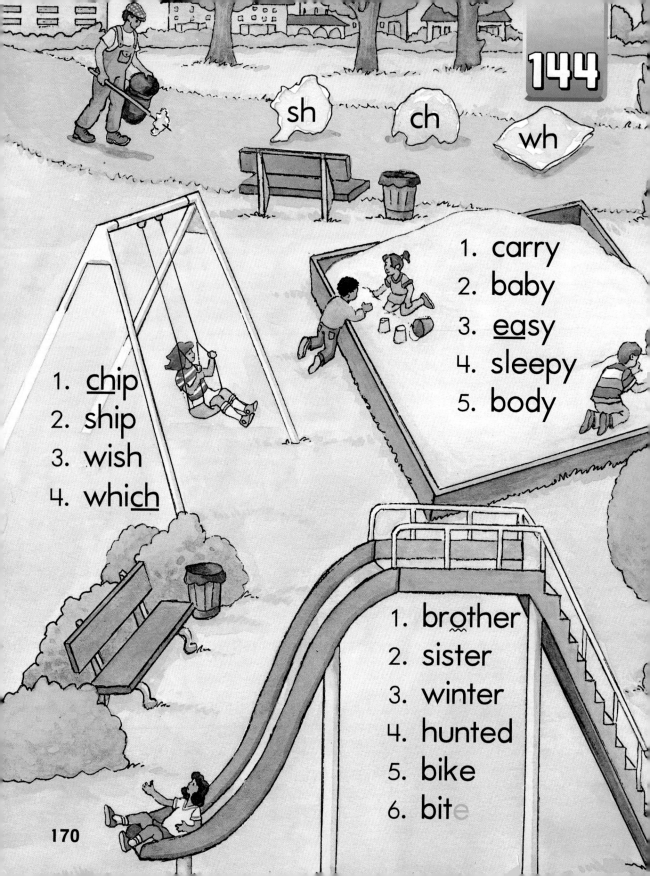

sh ch wh

1. carry
2. baby
3. <u>ea</u>sy
4. sleepy
5. body

1. <u>ch</u>ip
2. ship
3. wish
4. whi<u>ch</u>

1. brother
2. sister
3. winter
4. hunted
5. bike
6. bite

Pam and the Gold Robber

Pam lived on a ship that had a shop. A robber had a plan to take the gold that she had in her shop. The robber did not know that Pam's gold was not in a big lump.

The robber came to Pam's ship in a little boat. He got into Pam's shop.

As the robber hunted for gold, he said, "I see sacks and rocks and clocks, but I don't see gold."

Just as he was leaving, two cops grabbed him.
Later, the cops asked Pam, "Can you show us how
you hide the gold?"

Pam told one of the cops to pick up the big
lamp. He said, "I can't do it."

The other cop smiled. She said, "I know why.
That lamp is made of gold. Ho ho."

The end.

1. only
2. hurry
3. tiny
4. thank
5. sitting
6. swim

1. somebody
2. Jill
3. bite
4. brother
5. jumped

1. sister
2. leaves
3. leaping
4. turn
5. first

The Bug Who Bit
Part One

Jill was a bug who bit other bugs. That's
why her brother and sister did not like to be near
her.

One day she was playing with her brother
and sister. The bugs were leaping over leaves.

It's my turn.

Jill's sister jumped over three leaves. Her brother said, "Now it is my turn."

"No," Jill said. "It is my turn."

Her brother said, "I was here first. So it is my turn."

As he started to take his turn, he said, "Ow. Ow. Ow."

Why did he say that?

Somebody bit him.

Why can't we play?

Jill's brother and sister stopped playing. Her sister said, "We don't like to play with a bug who bites."

Her brother said, "Ow. I hurt."

So her brother and sister ran home.

Jill asked, "Why can't we play some more?"

More to come.

x b ar sh ch g

ol or

1. spring
2. snow
3. pants
4. winter
5. summer

1. I've
2. broke
3. <u>ch</u>omp
4. bigger
5. glad
6. seen

1. r<u>ea</u>ch
2. <u>wh</u>ite
3. sh<u>or</u>t
4. m<u>ar</u>k

We can dive from that tree.

The Bug Who Bit
Part Two

Jill made her brother and sister mad. Her brother said, "Jill bites if things do not go her way."

One day, the bugs were at the pond. Her sister said, "Why don't we go for a swim?"

"Yes, yes," her brother said. "And we can dive from that tree."

"Oh no," Jill's sister said. "We don't know what is in that tree."

Jill said, "If something mean is in that tree, I will bite it."

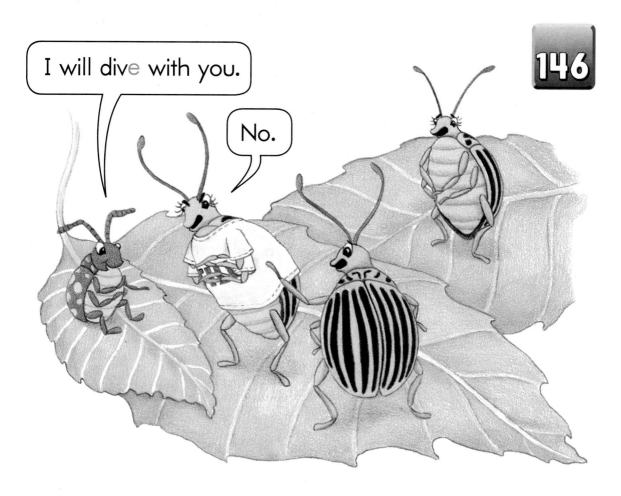

So the three bugs ran up the tree. The bugs came to a little tiny bug who was sitting on a leaf. That bug said, "What are you going to do?"

Jill's sister told him.

The little tiny bug said, "I like to dive. So I will do it with you."

"No," Jill said. "Leave this tree or I will bite you."

This story is not over.

b   er   ar   ch

1. bite
2. beat
3. bit
4. before
5. broke
6. bigger

1. chomp
2. hard
3. mark
4. white
5. beach

1. hiking
2. diving
3. biting
4. kidding
5. thinking

I can bite really hard.

The Bug Who Bit
Part Three

Jill told the little bug to leave the tree. She said, "Go away, or I will bite you."

The little bug said, "That is a mean thing to do. I don't bite other bugs, but I can bite really hard if I have to."

That's how h<u>a</u>rd I can bite.

Jill said, "Ho ho. You think you can bite
h<u>a</u>rd, but you can't b<u>ea</u>t me at bit<u>ing</u>."

Jill ran over to a stick and bit it. Her bite
made a little m<u>a</u>rk on the stick.

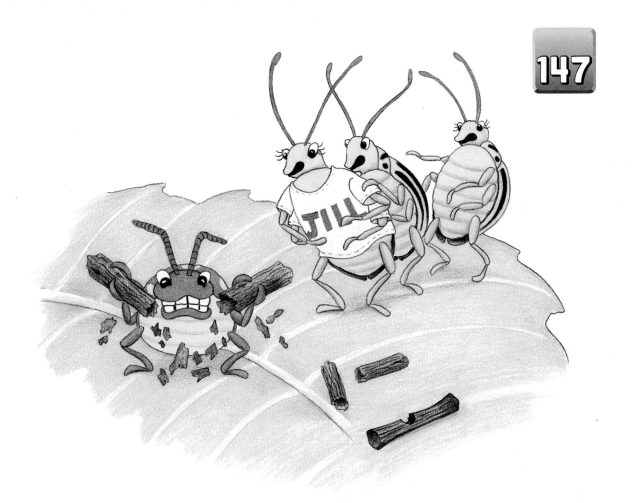

The little bug ran over to another stick and bit it. "<u>CH</u>OMP." His bite broke the stick.

Next, he bit a bigger stick. "<u>CH</u>OMP." That stick broke too.

Jill's sister said, "You can bite like no other bug I've seen."

Jill's brother said, "Yes, and I'm glad you don't bite other bugs."

More next time.

g   d   p   b   c

or
ol

1. before
2. somebody
3. sunburn

1. diving
2. biting
3. thinking
4. kidding

1. short
2. told
3. story
4. storm
5. rolling

1. hurry
2. hotter
3. birds
4. pants

My mom told me ...

The Bug Who Bit
Part Four

Jill had just seen a little tiny bug bite two sticks. The little bug said, "My mom told me not to be mean, so I try not to bite bugs. If a bug is really mean to me and makes me really mad, I bite."

Jill was thinking, "I will not make this bug mad at me." So Jill said, "I was just kidding before. I don't bite other bugs. That is a mean thing to do."

Jill's brother said, "Do you mean that, Jill?"

"Yes," Jill said. "Only a mean bug bites other bugs."

Later that day, the four bugs had lots of fun diving into the pond.

After that, one of the bugs said, "Why don't we go hiking?" And the bugs did that.

Those four bugs became pals. And from that day on, Jill did not bite other bugs.

The end.

What Jan Sings

Jan liked to sing, but she made her mother sick of her singing.

One day her mother spoke to Jan. Her mother said, "I like the way you sing, but you sing the same thing over and over. Can you sing other things?"

Jan said, "I like to sing the same thing."

Her mother said, "I will do something for you if you sing more than one thing. What can I do for you?"

Jan said, "Will you sing with me?"

Jan's mom said, "Yes."

Now Jan and her mother sing lots of fine things.

If you are near Jan's home, you can hear that singing.

The end.

Sid Cleans Up the Town

Sid liked things that were clean. But the town he lived in had lots of dirt.

Sid told his mom, "I will make this town clean."

His mom asked, "How will you do that?"

Sid said, "I will make it rain. The rain will clean the dirt away."

"But how will you make it rain?"

Sid said, "I will sing. What I sing will bring rain."

His mom said, "I don't think singing will make rain."

But Sid started to sing. In a little while, the sky got dark and lots of rain came down.

Sid's mom said, "I do not know what to think now."

Sid smiled and said, "I think the town is clean now."

And it was.

The end.

e   a   i

1. winter
2. spring
3. shirts
4. b<u>ea</u>ch

1. y<u>ou</u>r
2. six
3. week
4. bag
5. dock
6. black

1. they
2. ten
3. rent
4. went
5. left

1. <u>ri</u>ding
2. <u>hi</u>ding
3. <u>di</u>ving
4. <u>bi</u>ting

What Jan Makes
Part One

Jan liked to make things, but she made the
same thing over and over. On one winter day, Jan's
mom showed Jan how to make turtles from rocks.

Jan made the same turtle over and over. At last she had a pile of rock turtles.

Her mom said, "That pile is so big I can't see the rug. What are you going to do with these rock turtles?"

Jan said, "I will pile these turtles on the beach. Kids can play on the pile of turtles."

Make a sh<u>ir</u>t that is not the same.

On one spring day, Jan's mother showed Jan how to make a sh<u>ir</u>t. Jan made five more sh<u>ir</u>ts that were the same as the f<u>ir</u>st sh<u>ir</u>t.

Jan's mom said, "You have lots of sh<u>ir</u>ts that are the same. Why don't you make a sh<u>ir</u>t for somebody other than you?"

"I will do that," Jan said. "I will make a sh<u>ir</u>t for somebody who is bigger than I am."

More next time.

e

o

1. let
2. ten
3. get
4. they
5. men

1. went
2. rent
3. shirt
4. h<u>ur</u>t

1. dock
2. plant
3. black
4. trad
5. cup
6. your

1. before
2. cold
3. shore

Six moms can fit in that shirt.

What Jan Makes
Part Two

Jan's mom showed her how to make a shirt. Jan made the same shirt five more times. After she had made those shirts, she told her mom that she was going to make a shirt for somebody who was bigger than she was.

Three days later, Jan showed that shirt to her mom. Jan's mom said, "This shirt is so big that six moms can fit in it."

Jan said, "I didn't know the shirt was going to be so big. What can we do with this shirt?"

"I think I know," Jan's mom said. "Come with me and I will show you." And she did.

Now, if you go by Jan's home, you m<u>ay</u> see what Jan and her mom did with that shirt. The shirt is on a car to keep dirt away. It seems to be a fine fit.

This story is over.

e i o ar ch ea ai

1. men
2. let's
3. left
4. when
5. went
6. get

1. boating
2. swimming
3. kitten
4. started

1. wishing
2. fishing
3. tell
4. sell

1. lake
2. nine
3. day
4. store
5. each

Ten Men

Ten men liked to do things with each other. When one man went to a show, the other nine men went with him. When one man went to the store, the other nine men went with him.

One day, a man said, "Let's go fishing."

The other nine men said, "Yes, let's go fishing."

So ten men got in a van, and away they went to the lake.

When they got to the lake, the men said, "We will rent a boat." And they did.

Only one boat was left, and it was not a big boat. It was made for three men, not ten men.

The first three men said, "We will get in this boat." And they did.

As they started to leave the dock, the other men said, "We will get in this boat, too." And they did.

Did the boat hold the men? No.

So the ten men did not go boating and did not go fishing. Those men went swimming.

The end.

e a i

z d x b

1. them
2. bed
3. pens
4. red
5. mess
6. when

1. <u>y</u>ear
2. <u>traded</u>
3. <u>planted</u>
4. <u>sleeping</u>
5. <u>ki</u>ttens

1. rid
2. sal
3. much
4. Debby
5. week
6. cups

1. five
2. two
3. piles
4. next

Debby Makes Trades
Part One

Debby liked to trade things. She was a fine trader. She said, "When I trade, I end up with more than I had before."

One week, she traded her bike for other things. She got another bike and a sleeping bag and some cash.

3

4

She traded the sleeping bag for a cat that had nine kittens.

She traded the kittens for lots and lots of other things. She ended up with her cat, a bird, a ring, three pens, five fish, six cups, two clocks, and the bike she had at first.

She made another trade for some ears of corn. This corn was not gold like other corn. This corn was red, and brown, and black, and white. She traded some of the corn and planted some of the corn.

The next year, she had piles and piles of corn. Her mom's pals liked that corn. So Debby made a lot of trades.

More next time.

o e u sh ch ar

1. fine
2. sale
3. may
4. these

1. tell
2. sell
3. three
4. free

1. much
2. rid
3. rugs
4. mess
5. bed
6. them

1. white
2. trade
3. named
4. opened

Debby Makes Trades
Part Two

Debby planted some corn that was not gold. It was red, and brown, and black, and white. The corn came up the next year, and Debby made lots of trades. After she was done trading, her home was a mess.

Debby had piles of things on the rugs and piles of things on her bed. At last her mom said, "You must get rid of these things."

Debby said, "But when I trade, I get more than I had before."

Her mom said, "I will tell you how to get rid of these things. Sell them."

Debby said, "That is a fine plan."

So Debby had a sale, and it was a big one.

When the sale was over, Debby had three ears of corn, two pens, one fish, and a big pile of cash.

Debby's
Will sell or trade

Debby had so much cash that she opened a store. It is named Debby's. Debby will sell or trade. So if you have things you don't need, you may make a trade with Debby.

The end.